• Minehead • Dunster • Blue Anchor • Washford • Watchet • Williton • Stogumber •
Heathfield • Crowcombe Heathfield • Bishops Lydeard •

GW00684744

WEST SOMERSET RAILWAY

COUNTRY WALKS

FROM OUR STATIONS

Contents

Introduction	2
WALK 1 MINEHEAD TO NORTH HILL	3
WALK 2 DUNSTER TO MINEHEAD	6
WALK 3 MINEHEAD TO BLUE ANCHOR	9
WALK 4 BLUE ANCHOR TO DUNSTER	12
WALK 5 BLUE ANCHOR TO WASHFORD	15
WALK 6 BLUE ANCHOR TO WATCHET	18
WALK 7 WASHFORD CIRCULAR WALK	21
WALK 8 WASHFORD TO WATCHET	24
WALK 9 WASHFORD TO WILLITON	27
WALK 10 WILLITON TO WATCHET	31
WALK 11 WILLITON TO SAMPFORD BRETT	34
WALK 12 WILLITON TO STOGUMBER	37

WALK 13 SOGUMBER CIRCULAR WALK	40
WALK 14 STOGUMBER TO CROWCOMBE HEATHFIELD	43
WALK 15 CROWCOMBE HEATHFIELD CIRCULAR WALK	46
WALK 16 CROWCOMBE HEATHFIELD CIRCULAR WALK (2)	49
WALK 17 CROWCOMBE HEATHFIELD CIRCULAR WALK (3)	52
WALK 18 CROWCOMBE HEATHFIELD TO BISHOPS LYDEARD	54
WALK 19 BISHOPS LYDEARD CIRCULAR WALK	57
WALK 20 TAUNTON TO BISHOPS LYDEARD	61

Introduction

Welcome to our latest book featuring 20 country walks from West Somerset stations.

The initial idea of promoting walks from WSR stations goes back to an 8-page paper booklet by Stephen Edge in the early days of reopening. My parents, Ron and Audrey Short, then produced three pocket books between 1993 and 2000 covering 32 walks, which we have since revisited and updated.

We hope you enjoy doing the walks as much as we have. The walks cover varied and beautiful scenery around West Somerset, many affording lovely views of the Brendons, Quantocks and the Bristol Channel. Reasonable footwear is recommended as some parts can be muddy, and please bear in mind times of the trains to take you back.

All the walks in this book were checked in the Spring and Summer of 2015, however please note that land usage and fence lines can alter over the years.

Many thanks to Richard Brooks who helped check various Crowcombe and Stowgumber walks, our youngest son Lewis who could always be bribed with a pub lunch to assist with a walk, and to Colin Howard from the Minehead shop who has given us the support to produce the book.

Malcolm and Natalie Short
Taunton
February 2016

Key:
F.P. = Footpath
S.P. = Signpost

Walk 1

MINEHEAD

Minehead Station, Greenaleigh Farm, Burgundy Chapel, North Hill

3½ Miles (5½ km) or 4¾ miles (7½ km)

Circular walk. One very steep hill.

On leaving Minehead Station, cross over to the sea wall, turn left and continue along the sea front to the harbour. Along the way you will see the sculpture indicating the start of the South West Coastal Footpath.

Go past the harbour and on reaching the roundabout at the end of the car park, take the Culvercliffe Walk on the left up into the woods. After you reach the top of the slope you will join a path coming in from the left.

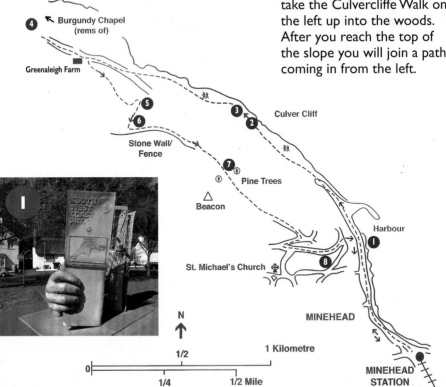

Continue ahead and after a short distance you will join an unmetalled road coming from the left. Keep right along the road and pass the National Trust sign for Greenaleigh Point. Along here on a clear day there are excellent views of South Wales across the Bristol Channel. Just before Greenaleigh Farm you will see steps on your left.

From here you may detour to visit the remains of Burgundy Chapel. Continue down through the farm and through the gate in front of you (S.P. for the chapel). Follow the path for approx ½ mile until the path forks. Go right down the steps and the remains of the chapel are in front of you. Little is known of its history, but it was probably erected by the Luttrell family for deliverance from shipwreck. Only

a stone doorway and part of a wall remains.

Continuing the walk go up the steps and onto the path which will take you steeply up past the farm. Cross the Coast Path diagonally

through a gate (a welcome seat on your right) and continue steeply upwards, S.P. Bridleway Moor Wood. On meeting the next crossing path turn right and continue for about 200 yards. On your left you will see a fence and dry stone wall. By a S.P. for North Hill, take the small path to your left through a gate which follows parallel to this boundary.

On reaching a group of pine trees you will find a gate and a sign for 'Bridlepath Minehead'. Notice the beacon in the field to your right. Go through the pines to a gate at the far end of the field by farm buildings. The view is magnificent!

Continue across the next field (farm buildings on the right) to

another gate, then keep down across the next field with the wood on your left. At the far end of the field cross over a stile into the woodland. Continue down the path with the fence on your right until you reach the road.

Turn right, then left. You will see St Michael's Church below. If you wish to visit the Church and Church Steps into the town, take the next road on the right (Church Road). Otherwise continue along Beacon Road.

Where there is a 'No Through Road' sign on the left, and the road bends sharply right, you come to the Coast Path. Follow the way ahead for the sea front down the zig-zag path. Nearing the bottom go through the second gap down a few steps, and keeping left come out between the pink and white cottages, opposite the start of the Coastal Path. Turn right for the station.

Walk 2

DUNSTER

Dunster Station, Alcombe Common, Higher Hopcott, Minehead Station

4½ Miles (7km)

A couple of steep hills.

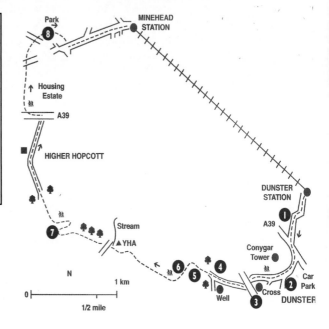

This walk gives splendid views over Minehead and the Channel on a clear day. Parts can be wet at times and waterproof footwear is recommended.

Leave Dunster Station and walk to Dunster village, as signed. (Use the underpass to cross the busy A39.) Pass the car park on your left, then turn right up a footpath at the top of the village just behind the Yarn Market. At a house called Priory Thatch take the footpath S.P. 'Private Drive Footpath Access Only'.

Carry on through three kissing gates, past the Community Orchard, to the Butter Cross.

Notice the Conygar Tower on the hill to your right, which was built as a folly in 1775 by Henry Fownes Luttrell. Conygar was the medieval for rabbit warren.

On reaching the Cross, turn left onto St. George's Street. Take the first turning on the right, Hangers Way, and follow the footpath for Grabbist Hill. As you walk up this (usually wet) track it is worth looking back at the view. Towards the top you will find St. Leonards Well on the left-hand side.

Go through the gate and turn right. Continue until the path forks and then take the left path, up through the trees (bridleway sign) keeping the remains of a stone wall on your left. On reaching the edge of the wood, go through the gate and straight ahead, keeping the fence on your right.

On meeting a crossing path, go through the gate, and turn right. Go straight ahead (not right) at the remains of a blue paint mark on a tree, and carry on downwards.

Follow the F.P. sign for the Youth Hostel (200 yds) and on reaching a road, turn right. Opposite the Hostel in the Vale entrance; turn left over the stream (signed Bridleway to Timberscombe).

After about one third of a mile, take a sharp right turn up through the trees and, where a path joins, turn steeply left to follow the edge of the field which is on your right.

Turn right at the top corner, keeping the hedge/wall on your right, and then turn right again, to go downhill. Continue down when you meet the road, and pass Higher Hopcott on your left.

On reaching the main A39 road, cross over and turn left. Before Odell Court, and just at the 40mph limit sign, turn right down a narrow footpath. Go straight across the next road and you will come out in a cul-de-sac. Keep right down the road and then follow a footpath on your left by a storm drain. You will come out opposite No. 34 on a road leading out of Minehead town centre.

Cross the road, turn right and, after 50 yards, turn left by the road sign down another path (marked for cycles). Cross yet another road to a footpath opposite and slightly to the left. In a few yards you will reach the Parks Walk. Turn right.

Continue down through the Parks, then turn left and continue down through the town shops until you reach Minehead Station.

MINEHEAD

Minehead, Dunster Beach (Dunster Station), Blue Anchor via Coastal Path

2½ miles (4km.) or 4miles (6½ km.)

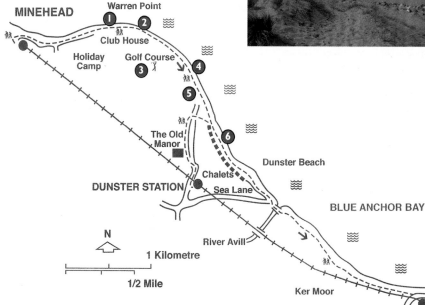

MINEHEAD

Warren Point

Club House

Holiday Camp

Golf Course

The Old Manor

DUNSTER STATION

Chalets

Sea Lane

Dunster Beach

BLUE ANCHOR BAY

N

1 Kilometre

1/2 Mile

River Avill

Ker Moor

BLUE ANCHOR STATION

This walk is especially good at low tide as there is easy walking along the sand.

On leaving Minehead Station turn right and walk along the end of the Promenade past the Holiday Camp until you reach the Golf Club.

Here you will find a footpath sign clearly marked on the end of the building as the coastal footpath. This leads along the beach on a stony track following parallel to the Golf Course (not on the Golf Course).

On a clear day there are delightful views of the bay and

across to South Wales. At the end of the Golf Course you will come to the chalets at Dunster Beach.

If you wish to return from Dunster Station, take the footpath marked on the right, between the old pillbox and the chalets. This leads through a wood, with a stream on your left. At the end of the wood, turn left and follow the farm track. A new footpath then runs parallel to the right of the old road, which will lead you around the farmyard. Here you rejoin the road which passes the Old

Manor Guest House. (This is an ancient building of particular interest. Part of the house is some seven hundred years old.)

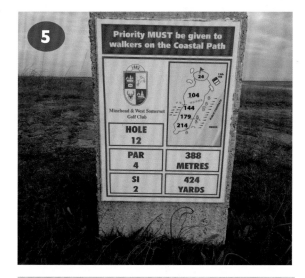

The path to Blue Anchor continues along the beach behind the chalets. Follow the signs around the bridge where the River Avill joins the sea and then continue parallel to the railway line. This will eventually bring you to Blue Anchor Station.

Refreshments can be found at the Café at Blue Anchor.

BLUE ANCHOR

Walk 4

T urn right out of the station to the sea front and then left along the beach in front of the chalets.

Continue along the shingle path until you reach a stile to cross the railway line.

A well-trodden path goes across the field towards the wood. Go over two stiles and at the second stile, after the wood, head for the gate in the far left-hand corner of the field where you will reach a track. Go through the kissing gate

---

Blue Anchor Station, Carhampton, Dunster Deer Park, Dunster Station

4 miles (6½ km.)

---

on your left and skirt the field with the hedge on your right. You will rejoin the track which leads up to the left by the side of Carhampton Church.

Turn right along the main road, opposite the Butchers Arms, for about 150 yards, cross at the lights, and take the first turning on the left. This is

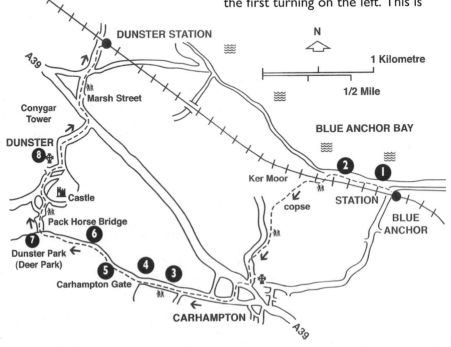

High Street, leading to Park Lane.

At the top of High Street turn right and continue along Park Lane. Keep right at 'The Court' and continue ahead to pass a No Through Road sign. Keep on up the hill. The road eventually becomes more of a trackway.

At the top of the hill go through the gate on the right, S.P. Dunster,

into the deer park. The path is well defined and leads down through the park with magnificent views of the Castle and village below.

On reaching the edge of the park, go through the gate and turn right past the cottages to the packhorse bridge over the River Avill (Gallox Bridge).

Continue ahead through a path by the bungalows, and here you may turn right to visit the Dunster Water Mill and Dunster Castle or left for the village.

Proceed through the village, past the church and Yarn Market as far as the main A39, where you will find an underpass to avoid the heavy traffic. Keep left and follow down the lane to Dunster Station

BLUE ANCHOR

Walk 5

O n leaving Blue Anchor Station
walk along the sea front as far as
'The Smugglers'.

Turn down the pub approach
road, keep right round the pub, past
the Home Farm reception and keep
straight down between the fences.

Skirt the three fields, going through
two gates, keeping the hedge and
stream on your right. Halfway down
the third field, when the hedge bends
to the right, keep straight on across
the field towards the farm house; here

Blue Anchor, Old Cleeve, Washford

2¼ miles (3½ Km.)

there is a small wooden stile at the
middle edge of the field.

Head towards the farm, keeping
the ditch on your left. You will reach
a wooden stile/bridge in the corner
of the field. Cross this and then pass
through the small wooden gate
ahead.

The path skirts
round the farmhouse
(Binham Grange).

Turn left on to the
farm path to reach
the house and garden.
A concrete path will
lead you down to the
Chapel Cleeve road.

Take the footpath
immediately opposite
which goes around

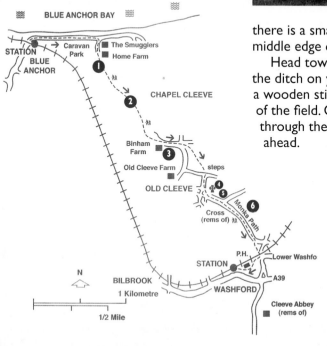

the back of the houses and through the kissing gate. Go diagonally right across the field towards the church.

There are steps in the corner leading to a very old lane, and the path climbs up to Old Cleeve Church. Turn left up steps into the churchyard. There is a well-sited seat in the churchyard which will enable you to sit and look back at the splendid view. Note the modern gargoyle (strictly a hunky punk) on the south-west corner of the tower, which has been carved in the likeness of a previous Rector, the Rev Hugh Allen.

Leave the churchyard by the south-east gate and turn left up the steep hill.

Bear right at the top (signed 'Washford') and continue uphill. You are following 'Monks Path'

which was used by the monks from the nearby Cistercian Abbey. (Notice the stones at the side of the road.) You will find the remains of a mediaeval cross at the top of the hill.

The road leads steeply downwards again and halfway down on your right is another footpath. This will take you to the railway line, and down steps to the bridge.

Go under the bridge. For Washford Station, take the path immediately on your right which follows the railway line and leads to the Washford Inn. If you wish to explore the village itself, the Abbey is well worth a visit.

Walk 6

BLUE ANCHOR

Blue Anchor Station, Daw's Castle, Watchet Station

4½ Miles (7km)

Coastal walk. Some moderate hills.

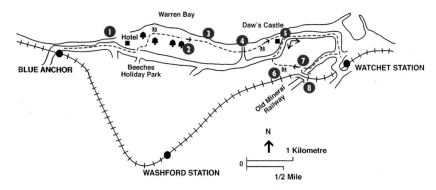

This is a delightful cliff and woodland walk and includes Daw's castle which was the likely site of the Watchet Mint and also a refuge against Viking attacks in the time of Alfred the Great.

Turn right out of the Station and walk along the sea front. Continue up past the Blue Anchor Hotel on the Watchet road. You will see a sign for a Permissive Footpath on your left,

S.P. Coastal Path. Take this and follow parallel to the road.

Follow the footpath into the wood, keeping left. It leads downwards through the trees for some way and eventually joins the old cliff path. Here turn right and follow the Permissive F.P. sign West Somerset Coast Path.

The path continues through the wood following the signs. Eventually you will catch glimpses of the sea below. The path comes out on top of the cliff at the edge of a field. Follow the footpath along the edge of the fields through two kissing gates until you reach a wood. You will find that the path comes out to the cliff edge several times before leading away.

Walk down out of the wood through a kissing gate into a camping field. Cross a short distance to the F.P. sign on the left. Turn left here and then keep ahead into the woods again, passing the path to the beach on your left, until you eventually cross a concrete track. Follow the sign for Watchet along the footpath.

Keep to the left around the caravan field, in between the hedge and the fence as the path leads uphill through a kissing gate into the woods. At the top, continue until you see the path going down to a gate and signs below. Skirt left around the

remains of Daw's Castle, through a metal kissing gate until you reach the road.

Here you may follow the road down into Watchet.

Alternatively, on reaching the road, turn right. Take care – this is a very busy road.

Keep up the road for approx 100 yards. Just past the right-hand bend at the top of the hill you will see a stile down on your left (F.P. sign). There are some steep steps here. Follow the path round to your left and over two stiles. You will see the former Paper Mill and the railway on your right. Go diagonally down across the field to a gate and stile in the corner, by the railway bridge.

Turn left here onto the track of the old Mineral Railway which will take you into the centre of Watchet, and the station.

WASHFORD

Washford Station, Bilbrook, Old Cleeve

5 miles (8km)

Circular walk. One steep hill.

This walk includes lovely views towards Exmoor and also the coast.

Leave Washford Station and follow the main road to the left around past the Washford Inn. Cross over the road at the Service Station and follow the path to the left of the garage. (F.P. sign).

Cross the stile in the corner to the left of the garages and follow the path bearing up left to a second stile by the wood. After a further stile continue ahead along the top of the field and climb over the step stile. Keep the hedge on your left, then continue ahead through a gateway along a track until you reach the road.

Cross over and follow the sign for Croydon Hall. Keep on, past 'Thistlewell' on your right, until you reach the next property, a white bungalow called Forches Garden, and a signpost in a grass triangle.

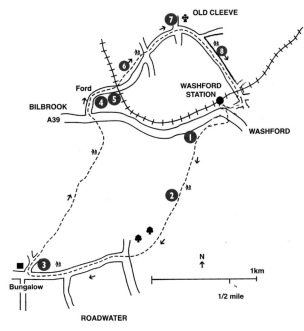

Take the right-hand fork and turn right down a green lane. Keep down the green lane which narrows part of the way down. On reaching the field go left down the F.P.. At the end of the enclosed path, cross the stile and continue down the field with the hedge on the left. (Note Old Cleeve Church in the distance ahead, and St. Decuman's Church at Watchet away on the right.)

Cross over the stile and take the enclosed path leading through the banks, which may be a little muddy after a period of rain and can be rather overgrown in places.

On reaching the opening and crossing of paths, continue down the edge of the left-hand field keeping the trees on your right, and then where the trees bend to the right, at the narrowest point of the field, follow the path to the left down across to the other side of the field to reach the busy A39 at Bilbrook through a gate in the far left-hand corner.

Cross the road with care, turn left over the brook, then take the first turning on the right and continue to the ford. Follow the path along the ford, then climb the path on the left under the railway bridge and up into the field. Keep to the right-hand side of the field and this will lead you to the Washford to Blue Anchor road.

Go straight across, and take the road for Old Cleeve, following it up to the church. (It is worth while pausing here to visit the church

and admire the view from the churchyard.)

Leave the churchyard by the south-east gate and turn left up the steep hill. At the fork continue right uphill (signed Washford). You are following the 'Monks Path' which was used by the Monks from the nearby Cistercian Abbey. At the top of the hill there are good views of the end of the Quantock Hills.

The road leads steeply downwards again and halfway down is another footpath. This will take you to the railway line, and down steps to the bridge.

Go under the bridge, and in 100 yards or so, take the next right into Castle Mead which leads you back to the Washford Inn and station.

Walk 8

WASHFORD

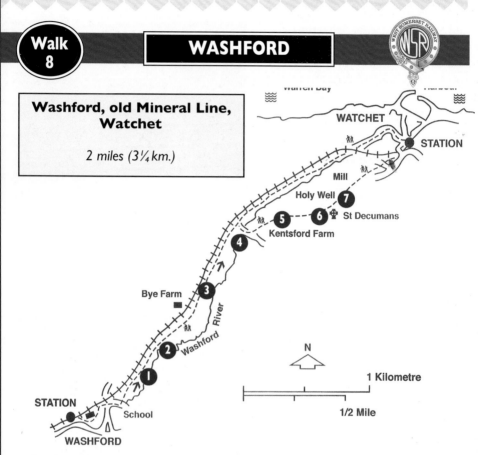

Washford, old Mineral Line, Watchet

2 miles (3¼ km.)

This is a short walk following the track of the old Mineral Line which leads from Watchet up into the Brendon Hills. Although all the rails were removed by 1919, the trackbed is still clearly visible in many places.

(An excellent small book of history and pictures is 'The Old Mineral Line' by R. J. Sellick).

On leaving Washford Station, turn left and follow a narrow path which leads between the car park of the Washford Inn and the first houses.

Turn left again at the end of the Inn and follow the path down and alongside the WSR line.

On reaching the road, continue across as far as the school, and then turn left down a small lane S.P. Mineral Line to Watchet, which leads to the Recreation Ground. The path runs parallel to the WSR line almost into Watchet and actually uses the track of the old Mineral Line.

Eventually you will come to Kentsford Crossing. On your right you will see Kentsford Farm, once Kentsford Manor, which was the home

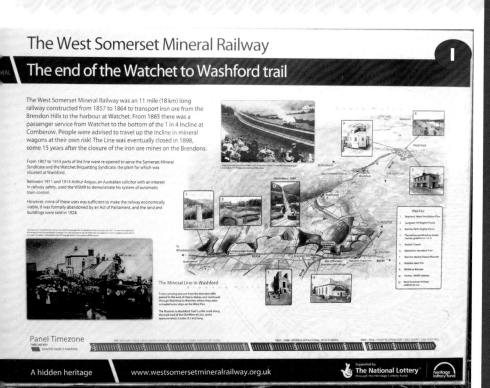

The West Somerset Mineral Railway
The end of the Watchet to Washford trail

The West Somerset Mineral Railway was an 11 mile (18 km) long railway constructed from 1857 to 1864 to transport iron ore from the Brendon Hills to the harbour at Watchet. From 1865 there was a passenger service from Watchet to the bottom of the 1 in 4 Incline at Comberow. People were advised to travel up the Incline in mineral wagons at their own risk! The Line was eventually closed in 1898, some 15 years after the closure of the iron ore mines on the Brendons.

From 1907 to 1914 parts of the line were re-opened to serve the Somerset Mineral Syndicate and the Watchet Briquetting Syndicate, the plant for which was situated at Washford.

Between 1911 and 1914 Arthur Angus, an Australian solicitor with an interest in railway safety, used the WSMR to demonstrate his system of automatic train control.

However, none of these uses was sufficient to make the railway economically viable. It was formally abandoned by an Act of Parliament, and the land and buildings were sold in 1924.

The Incline c. 1888

Map Key
1. 'Bearland' Wood Ventilation Plot
2. Langham Hill Engine House
3. Burrow Farm Engine House
4. The Incline and Winding House (incline gradient is 1 in 4)
5. Roadwater Chapel
6. Watchet to Washford Trail
7. Watchet Market House Museum
8. Watchet West Pier
9. WSMR at Watchet
10. Former WSMR stations
11. West Somerset Railway stations in use

The Mineral Line in Washford

Trains carrying iron ore from the Brendon Hills passed to the east of Cleeve Abbey and continued through Washford to Watchet, where they were unloaded onto ships on the West Pier.

The Watchet to Washford Trail is a flat stroll along the track bed of the Old Mineral Line, and is approximately 2 miles (3.2 km) long.

Panel Timezone

A hidden heritage | www.westsomersetmineralrailway.org.uk | Supported by **The National Lottery** through the Heritage Lottery Fund

---

of Florence Wyndham. A little way above stands the tower of St. Decuman's Church where in 1559 Florence, supposedly dead, was buried in the family vault. The story goes that in the night the sexton entered the vault to remove the rings left on her fingers, but on using a knife, blood flowed and the body stirred. The sexton, in great terror, rushed down the hill and threw himself into the sea, whilst Florence picked up the lantern and walked home to Kentsford.

There is a choice of ways here...

If you wish to visit the Church and St. Decuman's Holy Well, turn right, across the Washford river, through the

farm buildings, and then left over a stile, taking the path across two fields leading towards the Church. You will find the Well at the top of the hill on the left-hand side. From the Church a path leads down by the side of the old chimney right into the town, and comes out by the bridge over the railway.

If you wish to walk straight into Watchet (and avoid the hill) simply continue straight ahead along the Mineral Line and follow the well-defined path into the town. You will find the Harbour, shops and cafés. (For a direct route to the station go along Mill Street and Anchor Street.)

WASHFORD

Washford Station, Bardon Manor, Stream, Williton.

3 miles (5km.)

This walk starts from the far end of Washford Village, and as the main A39 is extremely busy and there is little or no footpath, the

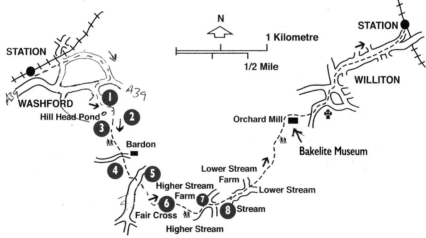

safest route is through the residential area.

On leaving the station, turn left and follow a narrow path which leads between the car park of the Washford Inn and the first houses. Turn left and follow the path alongside the railway line.

Cross the road, continue ahead past the school, and you will find the road goes uphill to the main road.

Turn right and then, a hundred yards or so ahead on your left, cross over to Quarry Road.

Walk straight up, between the bungalows and houses – F.P. sign.

Go up the path past the garages and continue past the back of the houses and more garages.

Take the footpath in the corner by a garage ahead on your right signed 'Bardon'.

Skirt the left-hand side of the field (you will see Hill Head Pond surrounded by trees in the centre), turn right at the corner, then along the edge of the field and continue through the gap in the far south-east corner.

Go straight through and keep ahead down the left-hand side of the field to join a green lane at the bottom.

On your left is Bardon Manor. This is famous for the story of the white dove which, last century, flew repeatedly against a pane of glass in the attic window. On searching the attic, papers pertaining to the relations between Queen Elizabeth I and Mary Queen of Scots and the Babington Plot were discovered.

Go into the opposite field (F.P. sign on right) and, keeping the hedge on your right, continue round the field up the track until you reach the road (B3190).

Take the footpath opposite, go through the field to the corner, then over a stile. Keep straight across the second field. At the far side of the field turn left down the grassy path.

You will see Stream below, with Orchard Wyndham House behind it. Keep straight ahead with the hedge still on your right down to the foot of the hill, then around to the left, where the track will take you to Higher Stream Farm.

Take the footpath to the left

2

immediately past the farm house and this will lead by the side of the water to Lower Stream. Turn left through the gate onto the road.

By the left-hand side of the entrance to Orchard Wyndham House you will see a footpath marked to Williton. This follows through the park beside the stream

Keep left after crossing the stone bridge, right over the next gate, keeping the hedge/fence on your right into the trees, and the path will bring you out behind Orchard Mill.

Here you will find the small Bakelite Museum.

Continue down the path to Williton Church, turn left in front of the Learning Centre and you will be in the centre of the village.

The station is 10 minutes walk along the Bridgwater Road (Long Street).

There are various shops and pubs available in Williton for refreshments.

Walk 10

WILLITON

Williton Station, Doniford Beach, Watchet Station

2 ¼ Miles (3.5 km)

A splendid walk at low or falling tide. At high tide, keep to the Doniford to Watchet road.

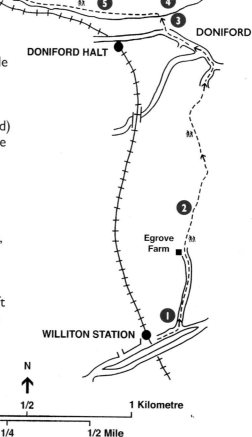

Leave the station on the east side across the level crossing (away from the village) and cross the bridge over the stream.

Turn left (F.P. signed to Doniford) and continue down the road to the farm.

Go through the yard and keep up right through a gate (look for the F.P. sign).

Follow a grassy path and cross over a stile on your right. Keep on, with a hedge on your left, climb over another stile and continue ahead.

Go through the gap on your left and walk diagonally straight across the field to the far corner. Here go over a gate and along a track between the houses to the road.

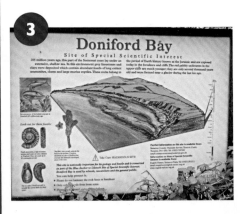

At the road turn left. Pass Court Farm and Doniford Farm and the remains of a stone cross. Where

the pavement ends by a small stone bridge, turn sharp right down the lane past Queenbee Bungalow. Take the path to the shore down the slipway with railings.

Cross the shore to the headland on the left, being careful on the wet rocks, where you will see steps. There are 72 to be climbed....

At the top turn left, then bear right across the field and head

for the furthest corner, towards the Lookout Tower.

The path leads alongside the railway line and past the Tower, down to Watchet Harbour.

There is a foot crossing over the railway line to the station platform on your left.

Refreshments are available at cafés or pubs in Watchet.

WILLITON

**Walk
11**

This walk provides peaceful paths and lovely views of the Quantock Hills.

Turn right out of the station and walk through the village, following the Minehead road.

Go right at the roundabout, then take the first turning left opposite Gliddons shop into Bridge Street.

Pass the old school on your left and then turn right for St. Peter's Church. Walk past the

---

Williton Station, Williton Church, Aller Farm, Sampford Brett

5¼ miles   (8 ½ km)

Circular walk. Two moderate hills.

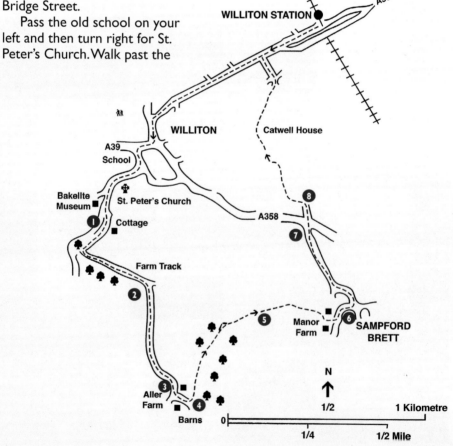

church, then straight on over the bridge, past the turning for the Bakelite Museum.

Bear left at the cottage in front of you following the F.P. sign. Climb the hill keeping straight on where the road bends to the left. (S.P. Aller Farm – Private Road.)

Keep walking up the track, around to the left, and past a seat to the top of the hill. At the top, turn right down the hill, still following the track down to Aller Farm.

Turn left down the track at the end of the wall, before the large barns (F.P. sign).

Pass the farmhouse on your left, and then turn sharp left at the corner of the barn. (F.P. sign).

Follow the path through the trees until the wood ends on your left and you see a footpath sign in front of

you. Take the path to the right, down through the wood. It may be a little muddy here in places.

Go through a kissing gate along the edge of a field, following the stream on your right. Follow the path across a bridge and past another kissing gate. Follow down the edge of another field, this time keeping the stream on your left.

Walk down to Manor Farm, through the gate and farmyard. On reaching the road, turn left into the village and at a signpost in the hedge turn left for Williton. Walk up the lane and cross the main road. You will see a footpath sign opposite.

Go along the track and cross over the stile. Skirt the field with the hedge on your left. Cross a further stile (or gap in the hedge) and again keep the hedge on your left.

Go through the black kissing gate to Catwell House and turn almost immediately right, in front of the house. Follow the path along the edge of the field.

Take the path between the houses and continue right through the housing estate to reach the main road.

Cross over and turn right for Williton Station.

Walk 12

WILLITON

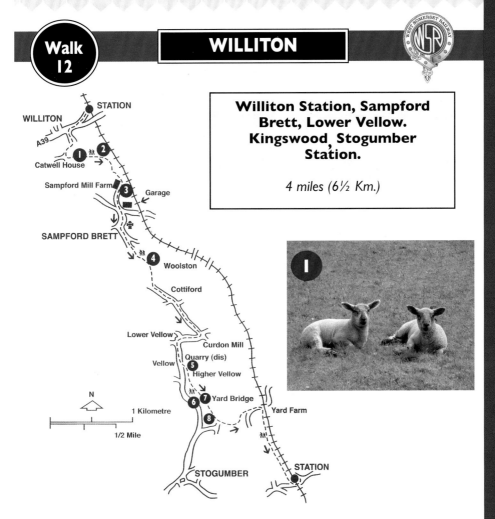

Williton Station, Sampford Brett, Lower Vellow. Kingswood, Stogumber Station.

4 miles (6½ Km.)

STATION
WILLITON
A39
Catwell House
Sampford Mill Farm
3 Garage
SAMPFORD BRETT
4 Woolston
Cottiford
Lower Vellow
Curdon Mill
Quarry (dis)
Vellow
5
Higher Vellow
6 7 Yard Bridge
8 Yard Farm
N
1 Kilometre
1/2 Mile
STATION
STOGUMBER

Leave Williton Station on the Minehead Road, and take the first turning on the left, through the housing estate (Townsend). Follow round the houses, until you find a narrow path between the gardens of houses Nos. 63 and 65 which leads over a bridge over a stream. The path will take you to Catwell House where several paths converge.

Go out of the gap and turn sharp left and through a narrow iron kissing gate then follow the boundary on your left-hand side. This leads around the base of the hill following the F.P. signs, then over a stile into a wood and a well-defined track through the farmyard.(Watch out for a vicious cockerel!)

You will come out at the garage on the main A358. This is a very busy road in the summer, so take care when crossing over to the lane opposite, signed 'Sampford Brett'. Bear left and past the church (or pause to visit, as there are some excellent carvings), and past the Village Hall on your right.

At the corner ahead, at the side of Brook House, you will see a footpath sign and then a second sign showing a parting of the ways. Take the right-hand track to Vellow which leads around the field past a bungalow then a house. Pass the house and follow up the hill to the right, through a small wood.

At the top of the slope walk down some steps, go through a gate and head across the field towards a pylon. You will join a green lane. Turn left and walk until you reach a road junction.

Follow the signpost for 'Stogumber' and after about 400 yards along the road you will pass Curdon Mill. Follow the road round right here to Lower Vellow where you will find the Vellow Pottery.

At the road junction, keep left for Stogumber and about a quarter of a mile ahead, on your left, you will find an uneven footpath, plainly marked, leading up through a wood.

Follow this along, steeply going up through a further wood and along the ridge of the hill, with the hedge on your right all the way. There are magnificent views of the Quantocks. Go through three fields until the path slopes down.

At the end of this field, just before it reaches a small lane, turn left along the edge of the field, keeping the hedge on your right, until you come to the remains of a gateway. This is some way round the field on the third side. Go through this, then over a stile, and then steeply down hill. At the bottom of the field go over a stile then down steps and turn right to the road.

Turn left towards the railway bridge, and then, just before you reach the bridge, follow the footpath to the right. This runs parallel to the line and will bring you to Stogumber Station.

Walk 13

STOGUMBER

Stogumber Station, Curdon Farm, Bicknoller, Meadowsweet Farm

4¼ miles (7km)

Circular walk.

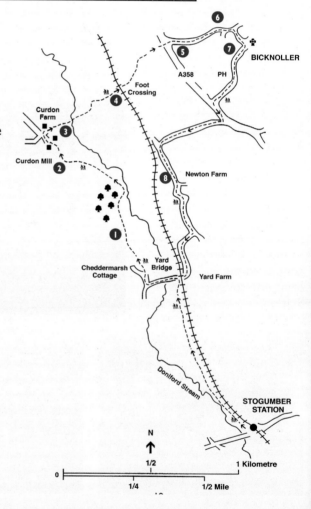

Leave Stogumber Station by way of the path down to what was the old Railway Hotel. Turn right, along the footpath which follows parallel to the railway line, to Yard Bridge, where you will meet the road. Turn left on to the road, cross the stream and then turn right at the corner house named Brambletye.

Following the footpath sign, go straight ahead through the gate and you will come to Cheddermarsh Cottages. Go in to the garden, turn right before the house, down steps and over the stile into the field. Turn left and follow along the edge of the field past some barns. Keep the hedge to your left and head for the corner of the field.

Go over the gate into the woods. Follow

the F.P. sign taking you right along the edge of the wood. Keep on through the field until you reach the back of Curdon Mill. Go right along the back of the Mill, through the yard and up to the road. Turn immediately right into Curdon Farm following the S.P. for Bicknoller.

Turn right just before the farm house, through a small metal gate in the corner of the yard, and head across to your right for the small bridge over a stream. Cross the bridge, turn left and go over a stile.

Go diagonally over the field to a large oak tree. Cross a concrete bridge over a brook, turn right and go over a stile into the field. Continue across the field until you come to a stile at the railway line.

Go over the line and walk half left up over the hill to end up by some

barns. Go over a stile. Bear left over the next stile then turn right and along the lane to come out on the main A358. Cross over and continue up Dashwoods Lane.

This will take you up to Bicknoller. Go past Combe Close, Gatchells Lane and bear right at the old school house to reach the church. Return down Church Lane, past the pub, to reach the main road again.

Cross the road carefully, turn left, then take a narrow lane to the right signed 'Newton and Kingswood'.

Follow this lane past Newton Farm and Meadowsweet Farm.

Take the next turning on the right and you will pass down under the railway at Yard Bridge. Turn left and return to Stogumber Station along the original track by the line.

STOGUMBER

This is a delightful walk along the valley between the railway line and Doniford Stream. It can be rather wet after a rainy period.

Cross the road from Stogumber Station, walk under the railway bridge and take the footpath on the left.

Stogumber Station, Water Farm, Roebuck Farm, Crowcombe Heathfield Station

3 miles (5km.)

STOGUMBER STATION
Water Farm
Leigh Cottage
Homeleigh House
Roebuck Farm
Roebuck Crossing
CROWCOMBE HEATHFIELD

N

0 — 1/2 — 1 Kilometre
0 — 1/4 — 1/2 Mile

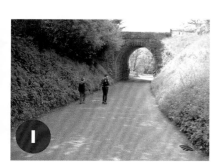

Keep left, above buildings, bearing left up a grassy track, and follow the railway line along, crossing over a couple of stiles and past a small plantation of trees.

The path and the line will go slightly apart, but on approaching Water Farm keep left towards the railway again (rather muddy here) and a farm bridge under the railway. Turn right in front of the bridge

and follow parallel to the railway above the farm to the road.

Turn right, and go left over the stile below the bungalow, just above the ford. The first field is divided by a fence.

Follow with the hedge on your right, go over the stile and then head towards the railway line and over a number of stiles. At the end of the third field go through an iron kissing gate in the hedge (note the unusual fastening) on to the lane above Leigh Cottage. Turn right down the lane. The path continues below the cottage through the gate on the left (F.P. sign).

Keep to the left, under the woods, but where the field widens go straight ahead between single trees.

You will come out on to the lane below the house ahead. (Homeleigh House).

Cross the road and over a stile, then keep straight ahead to a gate at the far end of the field the left-hand side, not the right.

In the second field, cross a small stream and follow around the hill to

the left, then cross the railway line through a metal kissing gate. Keep ahead but bear slightly to the left along the edge of the field, with the hedge on your right, to come out at the top of the farmyard of Roebuck Farm. Go through the metal gate.

Turn right, down through the farm and follow the drive under the railway bridge, until you reach the road. Turn left along the road which leads by the woods past Roebuck Crossing to Crowcombe Heathfield Station.

Walk 15

CROWCOMBE HEATHFIELD

**Crowcombe Station,
Roebuck Farm,
Crowcombe Village,
Roebuck Gate Farm,
Crowcombe Station**

4 miles (6½ km.)

Circular walk.

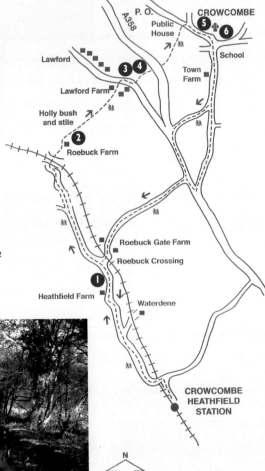

Leave the station by the north end and cross the railway over the bridge.

Continue along the lane, following in the direction of the railway, past Roebuck Crossing, as far as Roebuck Farm.

You will see a footpath marker on the right. Proceed down the farm track, under the railway bridge, and up the drive through the farmyard.

At the top go straight ahead through the gateway and turn sharp right. Go through a small wooden gate and up steps. Turn left through another gate and keep straight up left through the small gate opposite, then turn right along the side of the field.

You will find a little wooden stile in the hedge by a holly bush in the corner of the field. Turn right again, keep up and follow the fence along the field.

You will see Crowcombe Church in the distance. The path comes out at the left-hand side of Lawford Farm.

Turn right along the road for a few yards and then turn off left over a stile and on to a narrow path, just before you reach the stream.

Continue along the pathway, under the main road, and up as far as the village. You will come out through a small gate by the side of the Carew Arms.

Crowcombe village may claim to be one of the most delightful in Somerset. There is the Church House to visit and a wealth of heraldry and carved bench ends to see in the church.

Turn right, through

the village, past the school, and after Town End Farm, turn right down a narrow lane. This leads to the main Taunton to Minehead road. Turn left and walk along the grass verge for about 250 yards.

Alternatively pass the lane and carry straight on to the main road, then turn right along the grass verge for a short distance.

You will see an unsigned lane across the road, near a 50 mph sign which will lead you down to Roebuck Gate Crossing, and so back to the Station.

CROWCOMBE HEATHFIELD

Walk 16

Crowcombe Heathfield Station, Coursley, Lydeard St. Lawrence
5 Miles (8 km)
Circular walk (2).

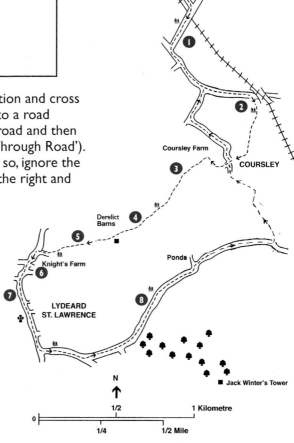

Turn south out of the station and cross over the railway bridge to a road junction. Turn left along the road and then keep left down a lane ('No Through Road').

After a hundred yards or so, ignore the road which bends round to the right and keep straight on towards a barn. The path leads downhill. You will come to a stile on your left and a little wooden gate on your right.

Go right through the gate and follow the path towards the railway. Just before the railway line, go right over a stile. Walk straight ahead across the fields, away from the railway line, following the line between two fields which will eventually become a hedgerow. Keep on to the end of the field, go through a small gap and turn right towards the farm buildings and in front of the renovated house. Go over the remains of the stile and you reach Coursley.

Pass through the gate and keep on through the farmyard. Go through the small gate and bear slightly left to a gateway at the far end of the field. Turn right through this gateway and shortly left into the next field. Initially keeping the hedge on your left, go over a number of gates and stiles (some overgrown) and then straight across the fields to the derelict barns in front of you.

Skirt to the right of the barns and keep straight ahead. Take the right-hand gate, through the field to an orchard and Knight's Farm. Turn left on to the road and walk through the village of Lydeard St. Lawrence. You will see the church on the right and then the school on the left.

At the end of the village take the turning left (unsigned) down past the houses. Follow this road past the sub-station, ignoring the turning on your right. After about a mile there will be a sharp left then right in the road and you will see a pond in the trees on your left.

Pass a concrete farm entrance and continue for about a third of a mile on the road. As the road steepens downhill you will see a gate and a F.P. sign on your left. Go through the gate and bear slightly

left up the field to a small gate in the hedge ahead.

Go through this gate and immediately turn right to go through another small gate. Bear left across this next field to join a track that descends via a gate and a stile into a small wood. The track will bring you out at Coursley Farm.

You may either retrace your steps across the field path, or take the road back to Crowcombe Station. (This comes out by the 'No Through Road' sign.)

Refreshments are available at the station when manned.

Walk 17

CROWCOMBE HEATHFIELD

This walk takes you to the highest point of the Quantocks.
Turn right out of the station and walk up the approach road to the bridge. Turn right over the bridge then follow the road around until it bears right for Lydeard St. Lawrence.

Here keep left down the unsigned lane. Go straight down, signed 'No Through Road'.

Keeping the barn on your right, keep on down the green lane and pass under the railway bridge. Note that this section may be slippery and muddy at times.

Carry on along the lane until you reach the houses at Seven Ash. Bear left and carefully cross the A358 ahead of you. Walk up the road known as Kennel Lane, until you reach a T-junction at Stockham Cross.

Turn right past 'Wayside' then immediately left up a 'No Through Road'. Bear right at the grass triangle then

---

Crowcombe Heathfield Station, Seven Ash, Wills Neck, Triscombe

6 miles (9.5km)

Circular Walk (3). Steep climbs both up and down.

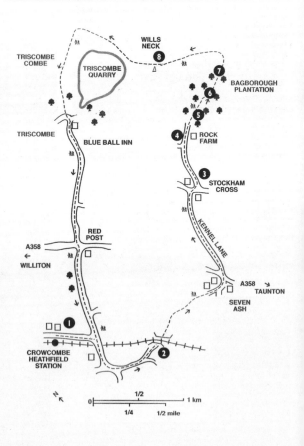

continue up past Rock Farm to the edge of the woods.

Go through the gate into the woods and take the right-hand path up Bagborough Hill. Cross the forestry track and carry on upwards.

At the end of the trees, walk out onto the common and then bear left along the main track on top of the Quantocks. This will eventually take you to the Trig Point at Wills Neck, the highest point of the Quantock Hills at 386m above sea level.

Take the right-hand track from Wills Neck which skirts around the top of Triscombe Quarry and follow it down to a gate.

Go through the gate and onwards (crossing a metalled road) past the historic Triscombe Stone, following the track. After about 350 yards go through a gate on your left and go down Triscombe combe to Triscombe itself.

On reaching the Blue Bell Inn, follow the road all the way to the main A358. At the Red Post junction, cross straight over to the grass verge, then bear left before taking the road back to Crowcombe Heathfield station.

Walk 18 CROWCOMBE HEATHFIELD

Crowcombe Station, Coursley, Nethercott, Combe Florey, Ash Priors and Bishops Lydeard Station

5 miles (8km.)

Turn south out of the station and then cross over the railway bridge to a junction. Go left along the road and then keep left down a lane. (signed 'No Through Road').

After two hundred yards or so, ignore the track to the left, and bear right with the metalled road (S.P. Coursley Farm). Follow this to the hamlet of Coursley.

With the cottage on your left, follow the track straight down to the wood, keeping the barns on your right. On leaving the wood, go over the stile and take the track upwards across the field aiming for the gateway ahead. At this point turn right up the hill, keeping the hedge on the left, to a metal gate in the top left-hand corner.

Go through the gate into a further field and straight ahead down the hill to the lowest point and a gate onto the Nethercott road. Turn left, walk through the hamlet, under the railway bridge, and then up the hill take the first turning right. This lane leads back over the railway to Combe Florey.

Just past the Farmers Arms pub you will see a footpath on the right in front of the bridge. Go alongside the stream to Combe Florey village. Continue straight ahead down the road by the side of the Manor, which was the home of Auberon Waugh.

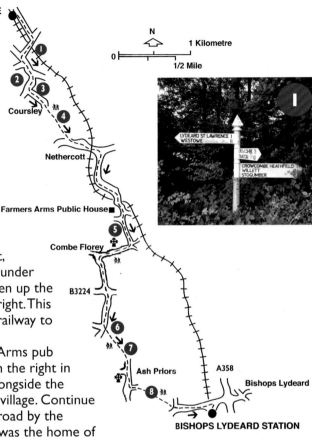

CROWCOMBE HEATHFIELD STATION

Coursley

Nethercott

Farmers Arms Public House

Combe Florey

B3224

Ash Priors

A358

Bishops Lydeard

BISHOPS LYDEARD STATION

N

0   1/2 Mile   1 Kilometre

On reaching the village, turn right and go past the village hall then up past the Manor gatehouse and the church. Follow the road up round to your left and you will eventually come out at a crossroads on the B3224.

Carefully cross the road and take the lane for Ash Priors and Halse. When a lane joins on the right, go over the stile by the second gate on your left. Go through the nearby metal gate then walk diagonally down across the field towards two oak trees and go through two wooden gates.

Still walking diagonally across the second field, head for the wooden gate in the middle of the fence. Go through this then keep diagonally up across the final field to another wooden gate. Bear right along the short lane and

over the stile to the road. This is Ash Priors.

Go straight down through the village past the church and the mill on your right and then turn left up the unmetalled lane by the side of a house called Highland Court.

At the end of the lane the

footpath takes you right between some open garages in the old farmyard. Go through the gate and diagonally across the fenced paddock. Go through the gate then head diagonally across two fields along a well-marked path. Finally turn left onto the road to Bishops Lydeard Station.

 Walk 19

BISHOPS LYDEARD

On leaving the station follow the signs to the village, crossing under the busy A358 by the subway. Continue ahead past the Lethbridge Arms. Notice the well-preserved Fives Wall with a Dutch gable at the back of the inn; there are very few remaining in Somerset. Fives was a handball game, very popular in the 16th Century.

Bishops Lydeard Village and The Whiskey Trail

2 miles (3km)

Circular walk.

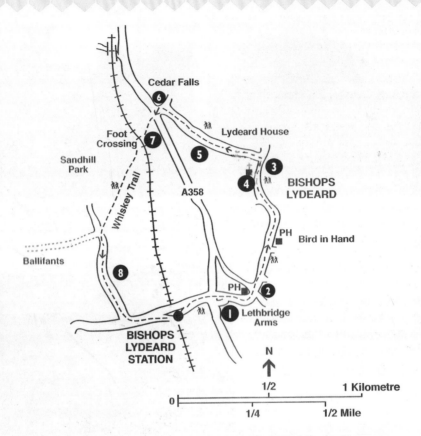

The Lethbridge Arms, named after a prominent local family, stands at one corner of Gore Square, the crossroads of the old Minehead road.

Continue down the hill, past Mill Lane on your right, and Frog House, so named because the road below this point used to flood regularly, leaving large numbers of frogs behind.

On your right is the village hall, with the village green behind, whilst on your left is a garage, just past which is the Health Centre and public toilets.

The road rises past the Bird in Hand Inn, the village War Memorial and the village school.

Continue past the library and village store to the church, which has one of the most beautiful towers in Somerset, housing a fine peal of eight bells. There are many treasures inside the church, including a complete 16th Century screen, and unusual carved bench ends of a ship and a windmill. Go past the church, then turn left on to West Street.

You will pass a big house on your right, mainly hidden from the road by a high stone wall. This is Lydeard

House, built in approximately 1740 and extended in 1787 to include a 'horsery' or stable block.

The road leads down to the entrance of Cedar Falls Health Farm, with its delightful grounds laid out with trees and waterfalls.

Carefully cross the main A358 to a grassy path opposite. This is known as 'The Whiskey Trail', from the days when American Forces were stationed at Sandhill Park, and would leave empty bottles behind them after a night out...

Cross the railway line at the foot crossing and proceed ahead, with the solar farm on the left and into Sandhill Wood.

You will come out of the woods onto the former road to Sandhill Park which has now been redeveloped into a private housing estate called Lethbridge Park.
Straight ahead is Ballifants Farm,

which was the childhood home of the science fiction writer Arthur C. Clarke.

Turn left onto the old road, through the woods, to the new houses and the former gatehouse. Turn left again onto the road to arrive back at Bishops Lydeard Station.

Refreshments are available in the village and at the station.

TAUNTON STATION

Taunton Station, Norton Fitzwarren, Cotford St. Luke, Bishops Lydeard Station

6¼ miles (10km)

A walk from the county town to the start of the WSR.

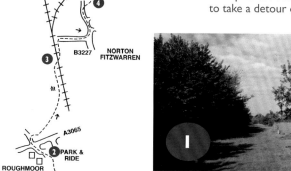

Note: At the time of writing, September. 2015, the section between Wick Farm and Cotford St. Luke is shown as closed due to two dangerous bridges. Hopefully the Council has plans to repair them and reopen the path, although there appears to be little wrong with them. In the meantime it is up to the walker's discretion whether to take a detour or not.

Turn left out of the north side of the station and cross Station Road to Railway Street. Follow the road round and then turn left along Rupert Street. By the corner of Leslie Avenue and Cyril Street West, turn sharp left down the footpath and cross the new footbridge over the railway.

Head up to the new roundabout on Staplegrove Road. Cross the main road and follow the bridleway sign next to the end house and walk down past the allotments.

Carry on through Frieze Hill Community Orchards and at the end of the orchard turn left down the slope to the pond. Turn right around the pond and head for the back of the white building at Roughmoor and you will come to the Park & Ride. Skirt round the left of the car park and take the next F.P. in the corner. Turn right into the lane then left at the T-junction. This takes you to the busy A3065 Silk Mills road.

Go straight across into Netherclay. After the brook take the F.P. on the right into the field. Follow the F.P. through the fields keeping the Norton Brook on your right. On reaching the footbridge, go over the stile then through the kissing gate and up over the railway. Go down and keep along the narrow path next to the railway fence. Turn right down Station Road into Norton Fitzwarren.

On reaching the main road through the village, cross over and turn left. Carry on past the bus stop and Manor Lane until the footpath ends in the housing estate. Go across into Manor Gardens (F.P.

sign) and continue up the footpath with the stream on your left and allotments on your right.

Go over the wooden footbridge and bear right along the right-hand edge of the field. Continue into the trees and cross the railway line. Cross the footbridge and take the right-hand path. Go through two fields. In a corner of the second field go over a stile onto the road. Turn right and follow the road until you see the new covered reservoir on your left, opposite a bungalow.

If the path is shown as closed, the only alternative route is to go back along the road as far as the B3227, turning right along the main road, then turning right again to Cotford St. Luke.

For the original route, follow the F.P. sign and go right up around the

top end of the reservoir. As you start going down the other side of the reservoir, take the F.P. sign through the gate on your right. Head straight across the field to a gateway in the hedge. Go into the next field and bear left towards a stile and bridge over a stream.

Go over these into the next field and follow the path around the right-hand edge of the field. Cross over another footbridge and across the field to the gate and the road into Cotford St. Luke.

Turn right and go up past the houses ('Access to South Villas and Dene Barton'). Continue up past the Community Hospital & Milsom Place, along the paths and roads, until you reach the other end of the road into Cotford St. Luke village.

Go straight over the road and down the marked F.P., to the road at Tithill. Turn left then right into the field, following the path along the left-hand side of the field.

Go over the footbridge at the bottom of the field, then keep straight ahead, keeping the fence, then hedge, to your right. On reaching the railway go through the kissing gates and across the line.

Follow the track up the other side towards the main A358. On reaching the road bear left along the F.P. This will take you parallel to the main road, and eventually Bishops Lydeard Station on your left.

Further Reading

This new edition of this popular Guide Book provides a background history of the line followed by a journey along the 22¾-mile line from station to station. Our journey takes us from Bishops Lydeard to Minehead calling at Crowcombe Heathfield, Stogumber, Williton, Watchet, Washford, Blue Anchor and Dunster.

The ideal memorable souvenir for those who have enjoyed the railway or to whet the appetite to visit this picturesque line to the seaside!

ISBN: 978 185794 478 5   £5.00

A new 7th edition of the popular Stock Book has been completely revised and updated and once again provides a detailed look at the locomotives and rolling stock based on the railway. Each locomotive is given a detailed review including details of the known history both before preservation and since being saved from the cutter's torch. The carriages in which visitors travel are described and details of the various types provided. The freight wagons are given due coverage and recognition. For those who enjoy trainspotting there is also a listing of all the numbers to underline in the traditional way!

ISBN: 978 185794 479 2   £5.00

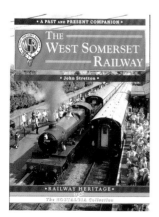

Two volumes taking a Past & Present look at The West Somerset Railway.

Volume 1
ISBN: 978 1 85895 166 9
£15.99

Volume 2
ISBN: 978 1 85895 258 1
£16.99

• MINEHEAD • DUNSTER • BLUE ANCHOR • WASHFORD • WATCHET • WILLITON •
STOGUMBER • CROWCOMBE HEATHFIELD • BISHOPS LYDEARD •

The ideal companion for those wishing to explore the Somerset countryside that surrounds the West Somerset Railway.

Here are 20 walks of varying lengths that start at a WSR station. Each walk description is accompanied by a sketch map of the route to follow.

On the map are also marked the key numbers for illustrations that have been taken along the walk and that provide reference points to guide you. These full-colour illustrations also provide an appetite-whetter for those planning to enjoy a walk as part of their visit to the

WSR. This book will also appeal to the 'armchair walker' who may not be planning a trip to the railway in the near future.

WEST SOMERSET RAILWAY
COUNTRY WALKS
FROM OUR STATIONS

ISBN 978-1-85794-480-8

£5.00